# The Sun and the Moon

## Written by Paul Shipton

Collins

You can see the sun shine in the daytime.

Do not look right at the sun.
It is bad for you.

You can see the moon shine at night.

On some nights the moon looks yellow.

On some days you cannot see
the sun because of clouds, but
the sun is still in the sky.

On some nights you can just see part of the moon.

The moon is round.

On some nights you can see all of it.

5

The sun seems to travel across the sky. At lunchtime, it is high in the sky. In fact, our planet spins around. This makes the sun seem to travel across the sky.

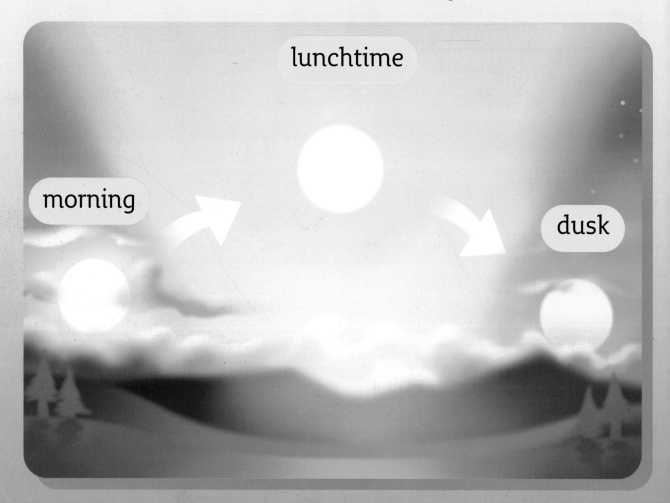

lunchtime

morning

dusk

You see the moon in different parts
of the sky at night.
This is because the moon travels
around our planet.

The sun is very big. It is made of very, very hot gas. The sun is a star.

Our planet travels around the sun.

The moon is not as big as our planet.
The land is very rocky.
There are no animals or plants.

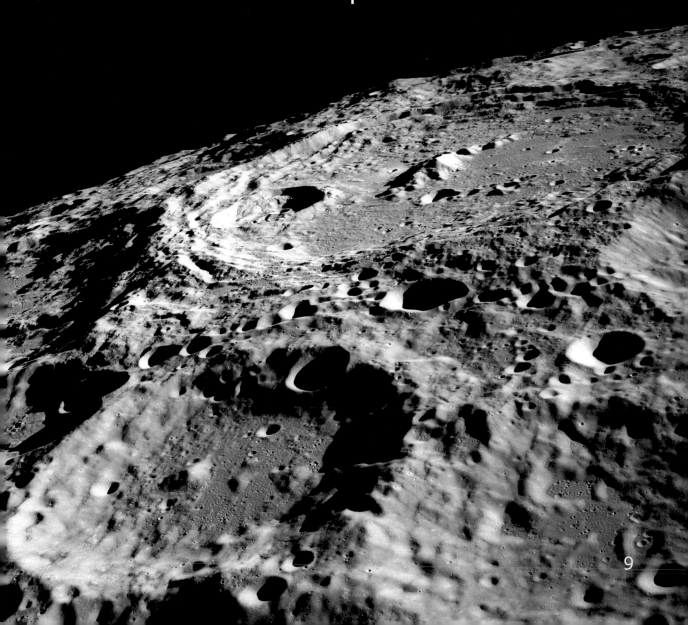

All of our light and heat comes from
the sun. The sun is much too hot to visit.

Some men did visit the moon in a rocket.
They stuck a flag up there.

This man is standing on the moon.

You can jump very high on the moon.
You can throw things a long way.

On some days you can see
the moon in the daytime, too.
It looks very pale in the sky.

You cannot see the sun at night, but you can see lots of different stars. They do not look the same as the sun because they are far, far away.

# The Sun

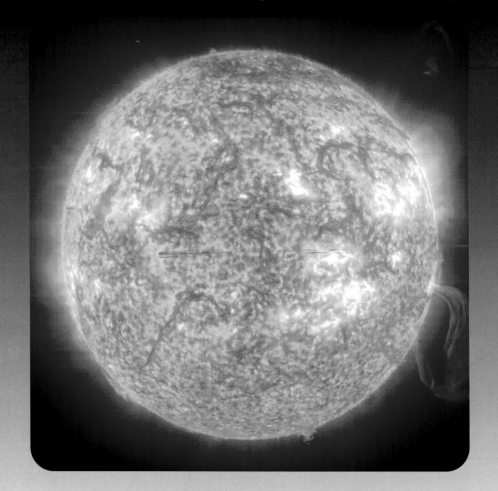

- You can see the sun in the daytime.
- The sun is round.
- It is made of very hot gas.

# The Moon

- You can see the moon at night.
- The moon is round.
- It is very rocky.

# Ideas for reading

**Learning objectives:** Blend phonemes for reading; Use phonological knowledge to work out and check the meanings of unfamiliar words and to make sense of what they read; Understand how information can be found in non-fiction texts to answer questions; Write labels and captions and begin to form simple sentences.

**Curriculum links:** Maths: Use language such as 'circle' or 'bigger' to describe the shape and size of shapes.

**Focus phoneme:** igh (high, right, night, light), y (sky), ay (daytime, away), a-e (make, made, pale, same), i-e (shine), y (very, rocky).

**Fast words:** the, to, all, you, do, some, because, there, no, come(s), they

**Word count:** 278

**Resources:** small whiteboards

## Getting started

- Write the words that feature the focus phonemes *igh, ay, a-e, i-e* and *y* on a small whiteboard and ask the children to fast-read them. If necessary, demonstrate how the "silent e" at the end of words changes the way the first vowel sounds, e.g. *The "e" at the end of "pale" is silent, but it makes the "a" sound longer, like "ay"*.

- Review the irregular high frequency words (fast words) in the book. Ask them to write these words on their white boards and to show you at the end.

- Look at the front cover together. What do the children think the book might be about? Is this is a fiction or a non-fiction book? Read the title together. What do the children already know about the sun and the moon?

- Point out that a non-fiction book does not have to read from cover to cover but can be dipped into to find pieces of information as needed. Ask the children what they think the book will tell them. Record their questions on the board.

## Reading and responding

- Give out copies of the book to children to read independently.

- Listen in on children to check they are blending words that feature the focus phonemes correctly and that they recognise the fast words in the text.

- When children have finished reading go back and look at the captions in the book. Point out that captions usually tell us more about the picture. Point out the capital letter and full stop. Ask children to find capital letters and full stops in other captions.

## Returning to the book

- Ask the children to read the book again as a group. *Which words did they find hard to read?* Ask children to demonstrate how they can blend through the phonemes in the words to read them.

- Look at the diagram on p6 and spend time talking about how the Earth spins. Choose a child to be the sun and another to be the Earth. Demonstrate how the sun and Earth move.

## Checking and moving on

- Ask the children to help you write captions for the picture on p8, e.g. *The sun is hot.* Scribe their suggestions on the board.

- Talk about the shape the full moon and the sun. Ask children to choose either the sun or a full moon and draw a picture of it. Ask them to write a caption for their drawings to describe the shape, e.g. *The sun is round.* Remind them to use a capital letter and full stop in their captions.

The sun is round.

## Reading more

*How to Grow a Beanstalk* (Blue/Band 4) is an instruction text that describes how to grow a bean plant. It also explains how the plant needs the sun to grow.

# Collins BigCat Phonics

# The Sun and the Moon

The sun and the moon shine in the sky.

Browse the complete Collins catalogue at
www.collinseducation.com

ISBN 0-00-723597-6

9 780007 235971

www.collinsbigcat.com

A simple non-chronological report